AF431347

Also by
Verna Gillis

I JUST WANT TO BE INVITED—
I promise not to come
(life as one-liners)
(2012)

I'LL NEVER KNOW IF I WOULD HAVE
GOTTEN THE SAME RESULTS
IF I'D BEEN NICE
Terror Firma
(2015)

TALES FROM GERIASSIC PARK -
On the Verge of Extinction
(2019)
live performance at The Colony in
Woodstock, NY, available as
an audio track

All titles available at amazon.com

FOR

Max, Ezri, Jonah, Tova, Kyla, Vida,
August, Leo, Jojo, Nico,
Marshall, Lila, Sarah, Ida, Finn,
Beatrice, Jamisen, Calvin, Adeline,
Shelby, Emmett, Xander, Soji, Rocket,
Igor, Bea, Thea, Cassius, Virginia,
Gustavo, Fiorella, Thea, Ben, Josie,
Emelia, Gina, Ramona, Delia, Isaac,
Cooper, Roxy, Nessa, Bird, Meira, Lulu,
Mia, Laszlo, Ruby, Harry, Phoebe, Theo,
Emilia, Vivie, Jack, Reid and Quincy

And to our extended families and friends
and neighbors in our quest to be the best
that we can be

Thank you to Linda Fite, Renee Gillis and
Kate McGloughlin for invaluable
suggestions and editing ideas. And great
friendship most of all.

With loving gratitude from in the
middle of somewhere!

The
I
of the
Storm

Verna Gillis
The Older

I was always emotionally available.
The problem was
which emotions

I have discovered the cure
for hypochondria:

Live long enough
and it all becomes real.

I often felt like the extra terrestrial.

Terminal vagueness was always his style.

Then it became his symptom.

I strive to maintain the distance
that says:

I will always be someone
not to be known by you

and you will forever remain
someone I do not want to know.

I was always tightly wired.

Pluck me with caution.

Operating on a high freakuency.

Final advertising campaign for a
failed product:

-Unavailable Worldwide

-Not coming anytime soon to a
store near you.

-You'll never know what
you never missed.

Platitude provider.

Covers all
and nothing.

Sometimes I think acceptance
is just a fancy word
for dissociated.

We keep going after what we never got
from the people who can never give it to us –

not too close for discomfort

It can only be better than expected.

We all seem to become
more of who we were
and less of what we've been.

My skin is rapidly separating
from my bones –
if I were to stand on my head
I would suffocate

However

if I could have stood on my head
my whole life
would have been different.

Everyone reaches their potential.

My mother bit me.
I bit my husband.

As you have been bit
so you will bite.

Tradition –
tradition

Perdition –
perdition

I have deep faith
in what
I don't believe in.

Trying to find the middle ground
between terror and despair.

Superficial intelligence
seems to be where it's at

The certitude
of the great uncertainty
is more certain.

The future:
closer to the present
than it has ever been.

Don't call me if you need anything!

Band names for Olders:

The Dry Vaginas

Los Impotentees

The Post Sexuals

Game of Groans

Horny comes,
horny goes.

Hemisfear –
Word by Tom Baschnagel

The side of the brain that rules

She introduced me
to her future ex husband,

the man with whom
their children would spend
every other weekend.

Humans are an endangering species

I can gauge my emotional health
by whether or not
I engage with telemarketers.

I got a case of delirium terrors

He threw me a perve ball.

Death is a life-changing experience.

Whistling in the light
Whistling in the dark

What exactly are you trying to catch
with bated breath?

Searching for the holy gruel...

If it's on my turf
it's on my terms.

Travel Insurance –

Bet on weather or not
you will survive your vacation.

It is only in the world
of medical reports,
that negative is positive,
and positive is negative.

We're all devoted to our just becauses.

Nothing gets created out of nothing.

Everything gets created out of something.

Go get your needs not met
from someone else

MODERN CURSES

(age 9 –to mother)

"May you turn into a rosebush
and then a donkey will eat you."

(age 7 - to father)

"I can't wait till you can't speak."

Do we really want our just deserves?

Speeding up to the STOP sign

Things often are
as bad as they seem.

Short term thinking
led to long-term consequences

What good is it going with the flow

if the flow is toxic?

I was great in pursuit.

Once it started I knew

It was the beginning
of the end.

And sometimes

it was only the end of the
beginning.

When things were good
I could always anticipate
how they would change.
And not for the best.

How selectively strange then
that when I felt so bad,
I could not imagine
it would ever end.

Never discuss politics with your surgeon.

Expert in the infinite varieties
of yearning and disappointment.

Everything is
as it never was.

It's so true what you're not saying.

Feeling too good?

Into a manic phase?

Wanna come down a notch?

Call me, I'll bring you down.

We were prime-mates.

One day it was a Rage Aria !

I toke my way into a better attitude.

The emotional manifest of fear
takes no prisoners.

I have spent an inordinate
amount of time in my life
in pursuit of minuscule hairs.

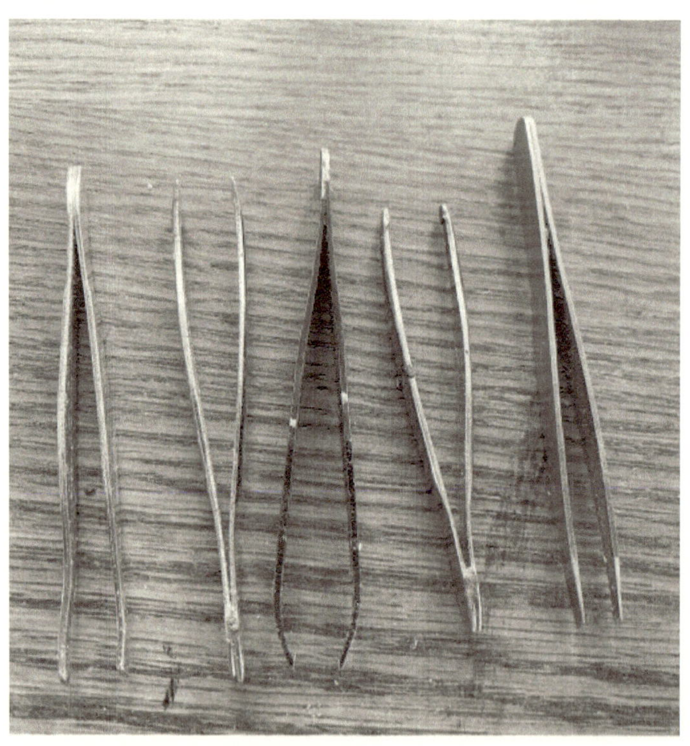

What not to say to an older person:

You've never looked better!

My mind doesn't work in mysterious ways

Once you finally get it,

that you can't buy love,

Life is much less expensive!

Some people are more better
from far further.

Family gatherings:

Regression Therapy

express track   -

right back

To all those still wounded

unhealed sad places

She is a spewer

a sewer spewer

pooh pooh her

that sewer spewer

It only takes one
to stop dancing

Women in menopause inhabit
their own portable sweat lodge.

No one will ever hear silence.

"On the precipice of discontent..."
-Ian Duncan

Some people are attached
to the idea
of non attachment

I'm overwhelmed
by underwhelm.

"I jumped into obsession and
now he owes me the life
I want to live."
    -Pinar Erdogdu

Hospice reminds me of Jehovah's Witnesses

Whenever you turn around
there's another pamphlet

If it's a pain in the ass,
go elsewhere.

I don't have any room in mine.

Viagra:

He is risen!

A reserection I can understand

One can never predict the past

We all come by dishonesty
honestly.

Dead.

End.

It took me a long time to realize
that dry and frizzy IS a hair style!

Totally redundant:

Therapy dog

Difficult relationship

Died suddenly

Horrorscopes

Aquarius: You will have a terrible day.

Pisces: You will obsess about all the "what ifs" and compare them to the "what isses."

Aries: One will turn the head, to check the incoming message indicated by the sudden lighting up of the phone screen, during sex.

Taurus: Your partner will find your stash of gluten products!

Gemini: The air will slowly leak from your emotional balloon.

Cancer: You will get an urgent message from your doctor's office to call them back immediately and have someone with you!

Leo: Your doctor will apologize profusely for having misdiagnosed you as lactose intolerant. Doctor suggests it might be emotional after all. O no!

Libra: You will commit to feeling sad by thinking about your ex.

Virgo: They will take away your credit card and cut it up in front of everyone on explicit direction from the credit card company.

Scorpio: You will forget that carrot cake is not a vegetable and you have once again gone off that diet that will never work.

Sagittarius: You will see his ex and she is happier and better than ever at the same time you are noticing his urine on the bathroom floor.

Capricorn: You will experience intense anxiety being separated from your iPhone for three cruel excruciating hours.

Why would anyone want to make the
most of a bad situation?

Making the least of a bad situation
is a much better idea.

Fear is my room mate.

Every morning when I get up
I acknowledge...

    Good morning fear

    I know you're here.

    We'll hang out

    Just not all day!

What difference does it make
that it won't matter in the end?

It matters now.

I was fear sighted

A damsel in distress married

A mansel in distress.

Together they created

A famsel in distress.

You can't be scared to death

And get to talk about it.

One doesn't get to reflect on old age.

There is no insurance

for pre existing conditioning

The future

Tense

Entitlements we learn

Are only for the rich.

Ain't that a bitch?

EXIT INN

Senior Housing Residence

Not everyone is yet or still alive.

Yet everyone who isn't

is still dead

My mind is stateless at the moment.

When one thing stops leading
to another,

you're probably dead

We'll all die.

Something you can bet your life on.

Obitchuary

word by Aram Rubenstein-Gillis

All the things one won't miss !

It's a lot
not to take in.

Conversation upon discovering a dead frog in the pool:

She to me:

        Tell me it didn't die.

        Tell me it didn't die.

Me to she:

        It didn't die.

Everyone's life is a real effort.
    -Renee Gillis

I have too much awaryness of the world.

Is there a road map for the void?

Anything IS happening!

Only the best of what happens
is for the best.

Up and addict!

I am the hostess

with the leastess.

Defrost and heat up

is what I do best.

What passes for love...

What stays for love...

I had to get over my interiorty complex.

Human life would die without us.

We do the psycho loco
And finally we knowko...

That's what it's all about.

March 5 2020
Kerhonkson, NY
In the Middle of Somewhere